SABRINA FAUDA-RÔLE

PHOTOGRAPHY BY AKIKO IDA

COOKIES IN A PAN

hardie grant books

Cookies for every taste

Classic cookies

Plain
6

Chunky choc
8

All-choc
10

Chocolate spread
12

Coconut choc
14

Salted milk chocolate
16

Nut cookies

Three nuts
18

Caramel Walnut
20

Hazelnut choc
22

Pecan maple syrup
24

Fruit cookies

Pear hazelnut
26

Fig, raisin, hazelnut
28

Speculoos apple
30

Raspberry almond
32

Date almond
34

Banana choc
36

Mango white chocolate
38

Blueberry pistachio
40

Cookies with a twist

Peanut butter
42

Coffee praline
44

Nougat cherry
46

Lemon marzipan
48

Cranberry oat
50

Orange oat
52

Lime coconut
54

Matcha white chocolate
56

Honey pine nut
58

Quinoa choc
60

Chestnut choc
62

Sesame
64

Special cookies

All coconut
66

Gluten-free
68

Vegan
70

concept
the cookie in a pan

what you will need
1 heavy-based 25 cm
   (10 inch) non-stick
   pan + 1 lid to fit
1 whisk
1 spatula or 1 large spoon

the stages
1 Mix the dry ingredients together.
2 In the pan, melt the butter over a very low heat.
3 Away from the heat, add the whole egg (and any other liquid
   ingredients), then whisk vigorously until well mixed.
4 Over a very low heat, add the dry ingredients then continue
   to stir with the whisk until you have an even texture. Smooth
   the surface with a spatula or spoon and cook for 10 minutes.
   The underside and edges of the cookie should now be cooked.

5 Add the fillings and decoration.
  Cover and cook for a further 5 minutes.
6 Remove the lid and wipe away any
  condensation that has accumulated, and
  then replace it. Allow to cool away from
  the heat for 15 minutes before serving.

tips

If you are cooking without a non-stick pan,
line the bottom of your pan with baking paper
before starting stage 2 of the process. To
make small cookies, prepare the dough in the
same way up to stage 3 and then, over a low
heat, add the dry ingredients and stir with
the whisk until you have an even texture.
Transfer into a bowl and then spoon the dough
into the pan in heaps. Gently spread them
apart then cook as before, but reduce the
cooking a little (5 minutes + 3 minutes).
Repeat until you have used up all the dough.

Plain cookie

using a 25 cm (10 inch) pan
serves 6

preparation: 5 minutes
cooking: 15 minutes
resting: 15 minutes

the dough

150 g (5 oz/1 cup) plain
  (all-purpose) flour
1 teaspoon baking powder
80 g (3 oz/⅓ cup) sugar
100 g (3½ oz/generous
  ⅓ cup) salted butter
1 egg

Mix together the flour, baking powder and sugar.
In the pan, melt the butter over a very low heat then,
away from the heat, add the egg. Whisk vigorously.

Over a very low heat, add the dry ingredients, then continue
to stir with the whisk until you have an even texture.

Smooth the surface and cook for 10 minutes. Cover and cook
for a further 5 minutes. Allow to cool for 15 minutes
with the lid on and away from the heat before serving.

Chunky choc cookie

using a 25 cm (10 inch) pan
serves 6

preparation: 5 minutes
cooking: 15 minutes
resting: 15 minutes

the dough
150 g (5 oz/1 cup) plain
   (all-purpose) flour
1 teaspoon baking powder
90 g (3¼ oz/⅓ cup) sugar
100 g (3½ oz/generous
   ⅓ cup) salted butter
1 egg

the topping
120 g (4 oz) squares of
   chocolate (choose white,
   milk, dark or a mixture)

Mix together the flour, baking powder and sugar.
In the pan, melt the butter over a very low heat then,
away from the heat, add the egg. Whisk vigorously.

Over a very low heat, add the dry ingredients, then
continue to stir with the whisk until you have an even
texture. Press the squares of chocolate into the dough.

Smooth the surface and cook for 10 minutes. Cover and
cook for a further 5 minutes. Allow to cool for 15 minutes
with the lid on and away from the heat before serving.

All-choc cookie

using a 25 cm (10 inch) pan
serves 6

preparation: 5 minutes
cooking: 15 minutes
resting: 15 minutes

the dough
150 g (5 oz/1 cup) plain
 (all-purpose) flour
1 teaspoon baking powder
2 teapoons cocoa powder
50 g (2 oz/¼ cup) sugar
3 tablespoons demerara sugar
100 g (3½ oz/generous
 ⅓ cup) salted butter
1 egg

the topping
50 g (2 oz) small chunks of
 chocolate (choose dark,
 milk, white or a mixture)

Mix together the flour, baking powder, cocoa powder and
sugars. In the pan, melt the butter over a very low heat then,
away from the heat, add the egg. Stir well.

Over a very low heat, add the dry ingredients, then continue
to stir with the whisk until you have an even texture.

Cook for 10 minutes, then press the chocolate chunks
into the dough. Cover and cook for a further
5 minutes. Allow to cool for 15 minutes with the
lid on and away from the heat before serving.

10
classics

Chocolate spread cookie

using a 25 cm (10 inch) pan
serves 6

preparation: 10 minutes
cooking: 15 minutes
resting: 15 minutes

the dough

100 g (3½ oz/⅔ cup) plain
   (all-purpose) flour
1 teaspoon baking powder
50 g (2 oz/½ cup)
   ground almonds
60 g (2 oz/¼ cup) sugar
80 g (3 oz/scant ⅓ cup)
   salted butter
1 egg

the topping

9 teaspoons chocolate
   hazelnut spread
2 tablespoons chopped
   hazelnuts

Spread a sheet of baking paper on a flat plate.
Put nine small spoonfuls of chocolate spread on the
paper and chill in the fridge for 30 minutes.

Mix together the flour, baking powder, ground almonds
and sugar. In the pan, melt the butter over a very low heat
then, away from the heat, add the egg. Whisk vigorously.

Over a very low heat, add the dry ingredients, then continue
to stir with the whisk until you have an even texture.

Smooth the surface and cook for 10 minutes, then press
the spoonfuls of chocolate spread and the chopped
hazelnuts into the dough. Cover and cook for a further
5 minutes. Allow to cool for 15 minutes with the
lid on and away from the heat before serving.

12
classics

Coconut choc cookie

using a 25 cm (10 inch) pan
serves 6

preparation: 5 minutes
cooking: 15 minutes
resting: 15 minutes

the dough

100 g (3½ oz/⅔ cup) plain
   (all-purpose) flour
1 teaspoon baking powder
80 g (3 oz/½ cup)
   chocolate chips
50 g (2 oz/½ cup) desiccated
   (grated) coconut
60 g (2 oz/¼ cup) sugar
80 g (3 oz/scant ⅓ cup)
   salted butter
1 egg

the topping

1 tablespoon desiccated
   (shredded) coconut

Mix together the flour, baking powder, chocolate chips, coconut and sugar. In the pan, melt the butter over a very low heat then, away from the heat, add the egg. Whisk vigorously.

Over a very low heat, add the dry ingredients, then continue to stir with the whisk until you have an even texture.

Smooth the surface and cook for 10 minutes. Sprinkle the remaining coconut on top. Cover and cook for a further 5 minutes. Allow to cool for 15 minutes with the lid on and away from the heat before serving.

Salted milk chocolate cookie

using a 25 cm (10 inch) pan
serves 6

preparation: 5 minutes
cooking: 15 minutes
resting: 15 minutes

the dough
150 g (5 oz/1 cup) plain
  (all-purpose) flour
1 teaspoon baking powder
60 g (2 oz/¼ cup) sugar
100 g (3½ oz/generous
  ⅓ cup) salted butter
1 egg
100 g (3½ oz/⅔ cup)
  chunks of milk chocolate

the topping
3 pinches of flaky sea salt

Mix together the flour, baking powder and sugar. In the pan, melt the butter over a very low heat then, away from the heat, add the egg. Whisk vigorously.

Over a very low heat, add the dry ingredients, then continue to stir with the whisk until you have an even texture. Press the pieces of chocolate into the dough.

Smooth the surface and cook for 10 minutes, then sprinkle with sea salt. Cover and cook for a further 5 minutes. Allow to cool for 15 minutes with the lid on and away from the heat before serving.

16
classics

Three nuts cookie

using a 25 cm (10 inch) pan
serves 6

preparation: 5 minutes
cooking: 15 minutes
resting: 15 minutes

the dough

150 g (5 oz/1 cup) plain
   (all-purpose) flour
1 teaspoon baking powder
2 tablespoons sugar
100 g (3½ oz/generous
   ⅓ cup) salted butter
1 egg
1½ tablespoons honey
1-2 teaspoons
   vanilla extract

the topping

2½ tablespoons almonds
4 tablespoons walnut halves
2 tablespoons cashew nuts

Mix together the flour, baking powder and sugar. In the pan, melt the butter over a very low heat then, away from the heat, add the egg, honey and vanilla. Whisk vigorously.

Over a very low heat, add the dry ingredients, then continue to stir with the whisk until you have an even texture.

Smooth the surface and cook for 10 minutes. Press the almonds, walnuts and cashew nuts into the dough. Cover and cook for a further 5 minutes. Allow to cool for 15 minutes with the lid on and away from the heat before serving.

18
nuts

Caramel walnut cookie

using a 25 cm (10 inch) pan
serves 6

preparation: 5 minutes
cooking: 25 minutes
resting: 15 minutes

the dough
150 g (5 oz/1 cup) plain
   (all-purpose) flour
50 g (2 oz/⅓ cup)
   buckwheat flour
1 teaspoon baking powder
75 g (2½ oz/⅓ cup)
   demerara sugar
75 g (2½ oz/generous
   ¼ cup) salted butter
1 egg

the topping
2 tablespoons salted butter
50 g (2 oz/¼ cup) sugar
50 g (2 oz/scant
   ½ cup) walnut halves

In the pan, melt the 2 tablespoons of butter with the
sugar. Add the walnut halves and allow to caramelise
for 10 minutes over a medium heat, stirring regularly.
Pour onto baking paper and allow to cool.

Mix together the flours, baking powder and demerara sugar.
In the pan, melt the remaining butter over a very low heat
then, away from the heat, add the egg. Whisk vigorously.

Over a very low heat, add the dry ingredients, then continue
to stir with the whisk until you have an even texture.

Smooth the surface and cook for 10 minutes. Press the
caramelised nuts into the dough. Cover and cook for a
further 5 minutes. Allow to cool for 15 minutes with
the lid on and away from the heat before serving.

20
nuts

Hazelnut choc cookie

using a 25 cm (10 inch) pan
serves 6

preparation: 5 minutes
cooking: 15 minutes
resting: 15 minutes

the dough

100 g (5 oz/1 cup) plain
   (all-purpose) flour
1 teaspoon baking powder
50 g (2 oz/½ cup)
   ground hazelnuts
70 g (2¼ oz/⅓ cup) sugar
100 g (3½ oz/generous
   ⅓ cup) salted butter
1 egg

the topping

50 g (2 oz) hazelnut
   milk chocolate
2 tablespoons chopped
   hazelnuts

Mix together the flour, baking powder, ground hazelnuts and sugar. In the pan, melt the butter over a very low heat then, away from the heat, add the egg. Whisk vigorously.

Over a very low heat, add the dry ingredients, then continue to stir with the whisk until you have an even texture.

Smooth the surface and cook for 10 minutes, then press the squares of chocolate into the dough and sprinkle the hazelnuts on top. Cover and cook for a further 5 minutes. Allow to cool for 15 minutes with the lid on and away from the heat before serving.

Pecan and maple syrup cookie

using a 25 cm (10 inch) pan
serves 6

preparation: 5 minutes
cooking: 15 minutes
resting: 15 minutes

the dough

150 g (5 oz/1½ cups)
    spelt flour
1 teaspoon baking powder
100 g (3½ oz/1 cup)
    pecan nuts
2 tablespoons sugar
100 g (3½ oz/generous
    ⅓ cup) salted butter
1 egg

the topping

50 ml (2 fl oz/scant
    ¼ cup) maple syrup

Mix together the flour, baking powder, pecan nuts and sugar. In the pan, melt the butter over a very low heat then, away from the heat, add the egg. Whisk vigorously.

Over a very low heat, add the dry ingredients, then continue to stir with the whisk until you have an even texture.

Smooth the surface and cook for 10 minutes. Cover and cook for a further 5 minutes. Allow to cool for 15 minutes with the lid on and away from the heat. Drizzle with maple syrup before serving.

24
nuts

Pear and hazelnut cookie

*using a 25 cm (10 inch) pan
serves 6*

*preparation: 10 minutes
cooking: 25 minutes
resting: 15 minutes*

the dough
100 g (3½ oz/1 cup) plain
   (all-purpose) flour
1 teaspoon baking powder
50 g (2 oz/½ cup)
   ground hazelnuts
70 g (2¼ oz/⅓ cup)
   demerara sugar
100 g (3½ oz/generous
   ⅓ cup) salted butter
1 egg

the topping
knob of salted butter
1 tablespoon demerara sugar
1 pear (150 g/5 oz), peeled
   and cut into 8 slices

In the pan, melt the knob of butter with the tablespoon of sugar. Add the pear slices and cook for 10 minutes, turning them over halfway through. Set aside on a plate.

Mix together the flour, baking powder, ground hazelnuts and remaining sugar. In the pan, melt the butter over a very low heat then, away from the heat, add the egg. Whisk vigorously.

Over a very low heat, add the dry ingredients, then continue to stir with the whisk until you have an even texture. Press the pear segments into the dough.

Smooth the surface and cook for 10 minutes. Cover and cook for a further 5 minutes. Allow to cool for 15 minutes with the lid on and away from the heat before serving.

Fig, raisin and hazelnut cookie

using a 25 cm (10 inch) pan
serves 6

preparation: 5 minutes
cooking: 15 minutes
resting: 15 minutes

the dough

150 g (5 oz/1½ cups)
   spelt flour
1 teaspoon baking powder
50 g (2 oz/¼ cup)
   demerara sugar
100 g (3½ oz/generous
   ⅓ cup) salted butter
1 egg
1 tablespoon honey

the topping

2 tablespoons whole
   hazelnuts
50 g (2 oz/¼ cup) raisins
2 fresh figs, cut
   into quarters

Mix together the flour, baking powder and sugar. In the pan, melt the butter over a very low heat then, away from the heat, add the egg and honey. Whisk vigorously.

Over a very low heat, add the dry ingredients, then continue to stir with the whisk until you have an even texture.

Smooth the surface and cook for 10 minutes, then press the hazelnuts, raisins and figs into the dough. Cover and cook for a further 5 minutes. Allow to cool for 15 minutes with the lid on and away from the heat before serving.

Speculoos apple cookie

using a 25 cm (10 inch) pan
serves 6

preparation: 10 minutes
cooking: 25 minutes
resting: 15 minutes

the dough

150 g (5 oz/1 cup) plain
   (all-purpose) flour
1 teaspoon baking powder
50 g (2 oz/¼ cup) sugar
100 g (3½ oz/generous
   ⅓ cup) salted butter
1 egg

the topping

1 tablespoon salted butter
1 tablespoon sugar
1 apple (150 g/5 oz),
   cored and cut into 8
20 g (¾ oz) broken
   speculoos biscuits

In the pan, caramelise the tablespoon of butter, tablespoon of sugar and apple. Cook for 10 minutes, turning the apple slices over halfway through. Set aside on a plate.

Mix together the flour, baking powder and sugar. In the pan, melt the butter over a very low heat then, away from the heat, add the egg. Whisk vigorously.

Over a very low heat, add the dry ingredients, then continue to stir with the whisk until you have an even texture.

Smooth the surface and cook for 10 minutes, then press the caramelised apple slices and pieces of speculoos biscuit into the dough. Cover and cook for a further 5 minutes. Allow to cool for 15 minutes with the lid on and away from the heat before serving.

30
fruits

Raspberry and almond cookie

using a 25 cm (10 inch) pan
serves 6

preparation: 5 minutes
cooking: 20 minutes
resting: 15 minutes

the dough
75 g (5 oz/½ cup) plain
   (all-purpose) flour
1 teaspoon baking powder
75 g (2½ oz/¾ cup)
   ground almonds
60 g (2 oz/¼ cup) sugar
100 g (3½ oz/generous
   ⅓ cup) salted butter
1 egg

the topping
80 g (3 oz) raspberries
2 tablespoons flaked almonds

In the pan, toast the flaked almonds for 5 minutes, stirring constantly. Set aside on a plate.

Mix together the flour, baking powder, ground almonds and sugar. In the pan, melt the butter over a very low heat then, away from the heat, add the egg. Whisk vigorously.

Over a very low heat, add the dry ingredients, then continue to stir with the whisk until you have an even texture.

Smooth the surface and cook for 10 minutes, then press the raspberries into the dough and sprinkle the flaked almonds on top. Cover and cook for a further 5 minutes. Allow to cool for 15 minutes with the lid on and away from the heat before serving.

32
fruits

Date and almond cookie

using a 25 cm (10 inch) pan
serves 6

preparation: 10 minutes
cooking: 15 minutes
resting: 15 minutes

the dough

100 g (3½ oz/⅔ cup) plain
  (all-purpose) flour
1 teaspoon baking powder
50 g (2 oz/½ cup)
  ground almonds
50 g (2 oz/¼ cup) sugar
50 g (2 oz/scant ¼ cup)
  salted butter
1 egg
100 g (3½ oz/generous
  ½ cup) chopped dates
50 ml (2 fl oz/scant
  ¼ cup) almond milk

the topping

4 dates, halved
8 coarsely chopped almonds

Mix together the flour, baking powder, ground almonds and sugar. In the pan, melt the butter over a very low heat then, away from the heat, add the egg, chopped dates and almond milk. Whisk vigorously.

Over a very low heat, add the dry ingredients, then continue to stir with the whisk until you have an even texture.

Smooth the surface and cook for 10 minutes, then press the date pieces and almonds into the dough. Cover and cook for a further 5 minutes. Allow to cool for 15 minutes with the lid on and away from the heat before serving.

Banana choc cookie

using a 25 cm (10 inch) pan
serves 6

preparation: 10 minutes
cooking: 25 minutes
resting: 15 minutes

the dough

150 g (5 oz/1 cup) plain
  (all-purpose) flour
1 teaspoon baking powder
70 g (2¼ oz/⅓ cup) sugar
100 g (3½ oz/generous
  ⅓ cup) salted butter
1 egg

the topping

2 bananas, cut into rounds
1 tablespoon sugar
1 tablespoon butter
75 g (2½ oz/scant
  ½ cup) chocolate chips

Mix together the flour, baking powder and sugar. Coat
the banana rounds with the tablespoon of sugar.

Heat the pan over a high heat and add the banana rounds
with the knob of butter. Allow to caramelise for
5 minutes on each side. Remove from the pan and set aside,
then melt the remaining butter over a very low heat.
Away from the heat, add the egg and whisk vigorously.

Over a very low heat, add the dry ingredients, then continue
to stir with the whisk until you have an even texture.

Press the banana rounds into the dough. Smooth the surface
and cook for 10 minutes. Sprinkle the chocolate chips on top.
Cover and cook for a further 5 minutes. Allow to cool for
15 minutes with the lid on and away from the heat
before serving.

Mango and white chocolate cookie

using a 25 cm (10 inch) pan
serves 6

preparation: 5 minutes
cooking: 15 minutes
resting: 15 minutes

the dough

150 g (5 oz/1 cup) plain
   (all-purpose) flour
1 teaspoon baking powder
2 tablespoons desiccated
   (shredded) coconut
50 g (2 oz/¼ cup) sugar
1½ tablespoons
   demerara sugar
100 g (3½ oz/generous
   ⅓ cup) salted butter
1 egg

the topping

½ mango, peeled and
   cut into strips
25 g (1 oz) white
chocolate pieces

Mix together the flour, baking powder, coconut and sugars. In the pan, melt the butter over a very low heat then, away from the heat, add the egg. Whisk vigorously.

Over a very low heat, add the dry ingredients, then continue to stir with the whisk until you have an even texture. Press the mango strips into the dough.

Smooth the surface and cook for 10 minutes, then press the white chocolate into the dough. Cover and cook for a further 5 minutes. Allow to cool for 15 minutes away from the heat with the lid on before serving.

Blueberry and pistachio cookie

using a 25 cm (10 inch) pan
serves 6

preparation: 5 minutes
cooking: 15 minutes
resting: 15 minutes

the dough

100 g (3½ oz/⅔ cup) plain
   (all-purpose) flour
1 teaspoon baking powder
80 g (3 oz/generous ½ cup)
   ground pistachios
   (or finely chopped
   unsalted pistachios)
80 g (3 oz/⅓ cup) sugar
100 g (3½ oz/generous
   ⅓ cup) salted butter
1 egg

the topping

60 g (2 oz) blueberries
2 tablepoons chopped
   unsalted pistachios

Mix together the flour, baking powder, ground pistachios and sugar. In the pan, melt the butter over a very low heat then, away from the heat, add the egg. Whisk vigorously.

Over a very low heat, add the dry ingredients, then continue to stir with the whisk until you have an even texture.

Smooth the surface and cook for 10 minutes, then press the blueberries into the dough and sprinkle the chopped pistachios on top. Cover and cook for a further 5 minutes. Allow to cool for 15 minutes with the lid on and away from the heat before serving.

40
fruits

Peanut butter cookie

using a 25 cm (10 inch) pan
serves 6

preparation: 5 minutes
cooking: 15 minutes
resting: 15 minutes

the dough

150 g (5 oz/1 cup) plain
   (all-purpose) flour
1 teaspoon baking powder
60 g (2 oz/¼ cup) sugar
1-2 teaspoons
   vanilla sugar
50 g (2 oz/scant
   ¼ cup) salted butter
1 egg
80 g (3 oz/generous
   ¼ cup) peanut butter

the topping

50 g (2 oz) chocolate-
   coated peanuts, chopped

Mix together the flour, baking powder, sugar and
vanilla sugar. In the pan, melt the butter over
a very low heat then, away from the heat, add the
egg and peanut butter. Whisk vigorously.

Over a very low heat, add the dry ingredients, then continue
to stir with the whisk until you have an even texture.

Smooth the surface and cook for 10 minutes, then sprinkle
the chocolate-coated peanuts on top. Cover and cook
for a further 5 minutes. Allow to cool for 15 minutes
away from the heat with the lid on before serving.

Coffee and praline cookie

using a 25 cm (10 inch) pan
serves 6

preparation: 5 minutes
cooking: 15 minutes
resting: 15 minutes

the dough

125 g (4 oz/scant 1 cup)
   plain (all-purpose) flour
1 teaspoon baking powder
70 g (2¼ oz/⅓ cup) sugar
50 g (2 oz) praline, crushed
3 teaspoons instant coffee
1 tablespoon milk
100 g (3½ oz/generous
   ⅓ cup) salted butter
1 egg

the topping

2 tablespoons crushed
   praline

Mix together the flour, baking powder, sugar and praline. Dilute the coffee in the milk. In the pan, melt the butter over a very low heat then, away from the heat, add the egg. Whisk vigorously, then stir in the diluted coffee.

Over a very low heat, add the dry ingredients, then continue to stir with the whisk until you have an even texture.

Smooth the surface and cook for 10 minutes, then sprinkle the praline on top. Cover and cook for a further 5 minutes, Allow to cool for 15 minutes with the lid on and away from the heat before serving.

Nougat and cherry cookie

using a 25 cm (10 inch) pan
serves 6

preparation: 5 minutes
cooking: 20 minutes
resting: 15 minutes

the dough

100 g (3½ oz/⅔ cup) plain
 (all-purpose) flour
1 teaspoon baking powder
50 g (2 oz/½ cup)
 ground almonds
80 g (3 oz/⅓ cup) sugar
100 g (3½ oz/generous
 ⅓ cup) salted butter
1 egg

the topping

100 g (3½ oz) cherries
 (defrost first if frozen)
50 g (2 oz) nougat

Mix together the flour, baking powder, ground almonds and sugar. In the pan, melt the butter over a very low heat then, away from the heat, add the egg. Whisk vigorously.

Over a very low heat, add the dry ingredients, then continue to stir with the whisk until you have an even texture.

Smooth the surface and cook for 10 minutes, then press the cherries and nougat into the dough. Cover and cook for a further 10 minutes. Allow to cool for 15 minutes with the lid on and away from the heat before serving.

Lemon marzipan cookie

using a 25 cm (10 inch) pan
serves 6

preparation: 5 minutes
cooking: 15 minutes
resting: 15 minutes

the dough

150 g (5 oz/1 cup) plain
   (all-purpose) flour
1 teaspoon baking powder
65 g (2¼ oz/generous
   ¼ cup) sugar
1-2 teaspoons
   vanilla extract
100 g (3½ oz/generous
   ⅓ cup) salted butter
1 egg
juice and zest of ½ lemon

the topping

50 g (2 oz) marzipan,
   cut into small cubes
2 tablespoons lemon zest

Mix together the flour, baking powder, sugar and vanilla extract. In the pan, melt the butter over a very low heat then, away from the heat, add the egg, lemon juice and zest. Whisk vigorously.

Over a very low heat, add the dry ingredients, then continue to stir with the whisk until you have an even texture.

Smooth the surface and cook for 10 minutes, then press the marzipan cubes into the dough. Cover and cook for a further 5 minutes. Allow to cool for 15 minutes away from the heat and with the lid on. Sprinkle the lemon zest on top before serving.

48
twist

Cranberry oat cookie

using a 25 cm (10 inch) pan
serves 6

preparation: 5 minutes
cooking: 15 minutes
resting: 15 minutes

the dough

50 g (2 oz/⅓ cup) plain
  (all-purpose) flour
1 teaspoon baking powder
100 g (3½ oz/1 cup)
  rolled oats
50 g (2 oz) dried
  cranberries
70 g (2¼ oz/⅓ cup) sugar
1-2 teaspoons
  vanilla extract
75 g (2½ oz/generous
  ¼ cup) salted butter
1 egg

Mix together the flour, baking powder, oats,
cranberries, sugar and vanilla extract. In the pan,
melt the butter over a very low heat then, away
from the heat, add the egg. Whisk vigorously.

Over a very low heat, add the dry ingredients, then continue
to stir with the whisk until you have an even texture.

Smooth the surface and cook for 10 minutes. Cover and
cook for a further 5 minutes. Allow to cool for 15 minutes
with the lid on and away from the heat before serving.

Orange oat cookie
with cream cheese

using a 25 cm (10 inch) pan
serves 6

preparation: 5 minutes
cooking: 15 minutes
resting: 15 minutes

the dough

70 g (2¼ oz/½ cup) plain
   (all-purpose) flour
1 teaspoon baking powder
100 g (3½ oz/1 cup)
   rolled oats
pinch of ground cinnamon
70 g (2¼ oz/⅓ cup) sugar
50 g (2 oz/scant
   ¼ cup) salted butter
1 egg
3 tablespoons cream cheese
juice and zest of ½ orange

the topping

3 tablespoons cream cheese
zest of ½ orange

Mix together the flour, baking powder, oats, cinnamon
and sugar. In the pan, melt the butter over a very
low heat then, away from the heat, add the egg, cream
cheese, orange juice and zest. Whisk vigorously.

Over a very low heat, add the dry ingredients, then continue
to stir with the whisk until you have an even texture.

Smooth the surface and cook for 10 minutes, then
sprinkle the remaining cream cheese on top in chunks.
Cover and cook for a further 5 minutes. Allow to cool
for 15 minutes away from the heat with the lid on.
Sprinkle the remaining zest on top before serving.

Lime and coconut cookie
with marshmallows

using a 25 cm (10 inch) pan
serves 6

preparation: 10 minutes
cooking: 25 minutes
resting: 15 minutes

the dough
150 g (5 oz/1 cup) plain
   (all-purpose) flour
1 teaspoon baking powder
50 g (2 oz/¼ cup) sugar
1-2 teaspoons
   vanilla extract
100 g (3½ oz/generous
   ⅓ cup) salted butter
1 egg
juice of ½ lime
1 tablespoon creamed coconut

the topping
20 g (¾ oz) marshmallow bits
20 g (¾ oz/⅓ cup)
   coconut flakes
zest of ½ lime

In the pan, toast the coconut flakes for 5 to 10 minutes, stirring regularly. Set aside on a plate.

Mix together the flour, baking powder, sugar and vanilla extract. In the pan, melt the butter over a very low heat then, away from the heat, add the egg, lime juice and creamed coconut. Whisk vigorously.

Over a very low heat, add the dry ingredients, then continue to stir with the whisk until you have an even texture.

Smooth the surface and cook for 10 minutes, then press the pieces of marshmallow and coconut flakes into the dough. Cover and cook for a further 5 minutes. Allow to cool for 15 minutes away from the heat with the lid on. Sprinkle the lime zest on top before serving.

Matcha and white chocolate cookie

using a 25 cm (10 inch) pan
serves 6

preparation: 5 minutes
cooking: 15 minutes
resting: 15 minutes

the dough

100 g (3½ oz/⅔ cup) plain
  (all-purpose) flour
1 teaspoon baking powder
50 g (2 oz/½ cup)
  ground almonds
1 teaspoon matcha
60 g (2 oz/¼ cup) sugar
80 g (3 oz/scant
  ⅓ cup) salted butter
1 egg

the topping

50 g (2 oz) chopped
  white chocolate
1 teaspoon matcha

Mix together the flour, baking powder, ground almonds, matcha and sugar. In the pan, melt the butter over a very low heat then, away from the heat, add the egg. Whisk vigorously.

Over a very low heat, add the dry ingredients, then continue to stir with the whisk until you have an even texture.

Smooth the surface and cook for 10 minutes, then press the white chocolate into the dough. Cover and cook for a further 5 minutes. Allow to cool for 15 minutes away from the heat and with the lid on before serving. Sprinkle the matcha on top before serving.

Honey and pine nut cookie

using a 25 cm (10 inch) pan
serves 6

preparation: 5 minutes
cooking: 20 minutes
resting: 15 minutes

the dough
150 g (5 oz/1 cup) plain
   (all-purpose) flour
1 teaspoon baking powder
20 g (¾ oz/¼ cup)
   ground almonds
50 g (2 oz/¼ cup) sugar
100 g (3½ oz/generous
   ⅓ cup) salted butter
1 egg
2½ tablespoons honey

the topping
50 g (2 oz/
   ⅓ cup) pine nuts

In the pan, toast the pine nuts for 5 minutes, stirring constantly. Set aside on a plate.

Mix together the flour, baking powder, ground almonds and sugar. In the pan, melt the butter over a very low heat then, away from the heat, add the egg and honey. Whisk vigorously.

Over a very low heat, add the dry ingredients, then continue to stir with the whisk to obtain an even texture. Sprinkle the pine nuts on top.

Smooth the surface and cook for 10 minutes. Cover and cook for a further 5 minutes. Allow to cool for 15 minutes with the lid on and away from the heat before serving.

Quinoa choc cookie

using a 25 cm (10 inch) pan
serves 6

preparation: 5 minutes
cooking: 15 minutes
resting: 15 minutes

the dough

100 g (3½ oz/⅔ cup) plain
  (all-purpose) flour
1 teaspoon baking powder
75 g (2½ oz/⅓ cup) sugar
75 g (2½ oz/generous
  ¼ cup) salted butter
1 egg
100 g (3½ oz) cooked quinoa

the topping

3 tablespoons
  chocolate chips (flakes)

Mix together the flour, baking powder and sugar. In the pan, melt the butter over a very low heat then, away from the heat, add the egg and cooked quinoa. Whisk vigorously.

Over a very low heat, add the dry ingredients, then continue to stir with the whisk until you have an even texture. Sprinkle the chocolate chips on top.

Smooth the surface and cook for 10 minutes. Cover and cook for a further 5 minutes. Allow to cool for 15 minutes with the lid on and away from the heat before serving.

Chestnut choc cookie

using a 25 cm (10 inch) pan
serves 6

preparation: 5 minutes
cooking: 15 minutes
resting: 15 minutes

the dough
100 g (3½ oz/⅔ cup) plain
   (all-purpose) flour
50 g (2 oz/½ cup)
   chestnut flour
1 teaspoon baking powder
3 tablespoons sugar
100 g (3½ oz/generous
   ⅓ cup) salted butter
1 egg
100 g (3½ oz/scant
   ½ cup) chestnut purée

the topping
50 g (2 oz/⅓ cup)
   chocolate chips

Mix together the flours, baking powder and sugar. In the pan, melt the butter over a very low heat then, away from the heat, add the egg and chestnut purée. Whisk vigorously.

Over a very low heat, add the dry ingredients, then continue to stir with the whisk until you have an even texture.

Smooth the surface and cook for 10 minutes. Sprinkle the chocolate chips on top. Cover and cook for a further 5 minutes. Allow to cool for 15 minutes with the lid on and away from the heat before serving.

Sesame cookie

*using a 25 cm (10 inch) pan
serves 6*

preparation: 5 minutes
cooking: 20 minutes
resting: 15 minutes

the dough

150 g (5 oz/1 cup) plain
   (all-purpose) flour
1 teaspoon baking powder
80 g (3 oz/⅓ cup) sugar
3 tablespoons sesame seeds
50 g (2 oz/scant
   ¼ cup) salted butter
1 egg
100 g (3½ oz/generous
   ⅓ cup) tahini
   (sesame paste)

the topping

1 tablespoon sesame seeds
2 tablespoons
   demerara sugar

In the pan, caramelise 1 tablespoon of the
sesame seeds with 1 tablespoon of the demerara
sugar for 5 minutes. Set aside on a plate.

Mix together the flour, baking powder, sugar and
the remaining sesame seeds. In the pan, melt the
butter over a very low heat then, away from the
heat, add the egg and tahini. Whisk vigorously.

Over a very low heat, add the dry ingredients, then continue
to stir with the whisk until you have an even texture.

Smooth the surface and cook for 10 minutes, then
sprinkle the remaining tablespoon of demerara sugar and
caramelised sesame seeds on top. Cover and cook for a
further 5 minutes. Allow to cool for 15 minutes away
from the heat and with the lid on before serving.

All coconut cookie

using a 25 cm (10 inch) pan
serves 6

preparation: 5 minutes
cooking: 20 minutes
resting: 15 minutes

the dough

100 g (3½ oz) coconut flour
50 g (2 oz/½ cup) desiccated
  (shredded) coconut
70 g (2¼ oz) coconut sugar
1 teaspoon baking powder
100 ml (3½ fl oz/scant
  ½ cup) coconut oil
2 eggs
60 ml (2 fl oz/
  ¼ cup) coconut milk

Mix together the coconut flour, desiccated coconut, sugar and baking powder. In the pan, melt the coconut oil over a very low heat then, away from the heat, add the eggs and coconut milk. Stir well.

Over a very low heat, add the dry ingredients, then continue to stir with the whisk until you have an even texture.

Cook for 10 minutes then turn the dough over onto a plate. Slide the cookie back into the pan to cook the other side. Cook for a further 10 minutes. Allow to cool for 15 minutes with the lid on and away from the heat before serving.

Gluten-free cookie

preparation: 10 minutes
cooking: 20 minutes
resting: 15 minutes

the dough

75 g (2½ oz/½ cup)
  rice flour
75 g (2½ oz/generous ½ cup)
  cornflour (cornstarch)
1 teaspoon baking
  powder (gluten-free)
80 g (3 oz/⅓ cup)
  demerara sugar
100 g (3½ oz/generous
  ⅓ cup) salted butter
1 egg

the topping

100 g (3½ oz/
  ⅔ cup) cashew nuts

In the pan, toast the cashew nuts, stirring constantly, for 5 minutes, over a high heat. Set aside on a plate.

Mix together the rice flour, cornflour, baking powder and sugar. In the pan, melt the butter over a very low heat then, away from the heat, add the egg. Whisk vigorously.

Over a very low heat, add the dry ingredients, then continue to stir with the whisk until you have an even texture.

Smooth the surface and cook for 10 minutes, then sprinkle the cashew nuts on top. Cover and cook for a further 5 minutes. Allow to cool for 15 minutes with the lid on and away from the heat before serving.

Vegan cookie

using a 25 cm (10 inch) pan
serves 6

preparation: 10 minutes
cooking: 30 minutes
resting: 15 minutes

the dough

2 tablespoons pure
   maple syrup
150 g (5 oz) almond purée
2 tablespoons plant
   milk (such as almond,
   hazelnut or rice)
100 g (3½ oz/⅔ cup) plain
   (all-purpose) flour
1 teaspoon baking powder
50 g (2 oz/½ cup)
   ground almonds
3 tablespoons
   demerara sugar

the topping

decoration of your choice
   (chocolate chips ·or
   squares, dried fruit etc.)

Mix the maple syrup together with the almond purée and milk. Add the flour, baking powder, ground almonds and sugar. Stir well until you have an even texture.

Shape into eight balls and flatten slightly. Warm the pan over a low heat and drop in four balls. Cover and cook for 7 to 10 minutes, then press the chosen decoration into the dough.

Cover and cook for a further 5 minutes. Allow to cool on a tray and repeat the process with the remaining four balls before serving.

First published by © Hachette Livre (Marabout) 2017
This English language edition published in 2018 by Hardie Grant Books,
an imprint of Hardie Grant Publishing

Hardie Grant Books (London)
5th & 6th Floors
52-54 Southwark Street
London SE1 1UN

Hardie Grant Books (Melbourne)
Building 1, 658 Church Street
Richmond, Victoria 3121

hardiegrantbooks.com

Text © Sabrina Fauda-Rôle
Photography © Akiko Ida

British Library Cataloguing-in-Publication Data. A catalogue
record for this book is available from the British Library.

Cookies in a Pan by Sabrina Fauda-Rôle

ISBN 978-1-78488-142-9

Photography: Akiko Ida
Layout: Frédéric Voisin
Text preparation and proofreading: Sabrina Bendersky

For the English hardback edition:

Publisher: Kate Pollard
Commissioning Editor: Kajal Mistry
Desk Editor: Molly Ahuja
Publishing Assistant: Eila Purvis
Translation: Gilla Evans
Typesetting: David Meikle
Editor: Kay Delves
Colour Reproduction by p2d

Printed and bound in China by Toppan Leefung Printing Ltd.